The History of Zimbabwe

From Stone Cities

to Modern Dreams

Introduction to Zimbabwe: Land of Ancient Wonders

Nestled in the southern part of the African continent, Zimbabwe is a land steeped in history and mystery. It is a nation that has witnessed the rise and fall of great civilizations, the construction of enigmatic stone cities, and the passage of countless generations. As we embark on this journey through the annals of time, we are drawn into a world where the past whispers its secrets through the ruins and relics that dot the landscape.

Zimbabwe's history is a tapestry woven from the threads of countless cultures and peoples who have called this land home. Long before recorded history, the region was inhabited by hunter-gatherer communities who left behind evidence of their existence in the form of rock paintings and tools. These early inhabitants, with their profound connection to the land, set the stage for the rich cultural tapestry that would later emerge.

The true wonders of Zimbabwe, however, begin to take shape with the rise of the Great Zimbabwe civilization. This ancient kingdom, whose origins are still a subject of scholarly debate, reached its zenith between the 11th and 15th centuries. The heart of this civilization was the awe-inspiring stone city of Great Zimbabwe, from which the modern country derives its name. This architectural marvel, with its massive stone walls and intricate passages, stands as a testament to the engineering and organizational prowess of its builders.

The Great Zimbabwe city was not an isolated phenomenon. It was part of a complex network of trade and cultural exchange that extended across the African continent. It played a pivotal role in the flourishing trade routes that connected the interior of Africa with the Swahili Coast and the Indian Ocean. Gold, ivory, and other precious commodities flowed through its gates, creating wealth and cultural exchange on a grand scale.

The decline of the Great Zimbabwe civilization remains shrouded in mystery. Some theories suggest environmental factors, such as deforestation and soil depletion, while others point to shifts in trade routes or political upheaval. Regardless of the cause, the legacy of Great Zimbabwe endures, leaving behind not only impressive ruins but also a sense of wonder and intrigue.

As we journey through the chapters of Zimbabwe's history, we will explore the diverse cultures and peoples that have shaped this land, from the Shona and Ndebele to the influence of Arab traders and European explorers. We will delve into the complexities of colonialism, resistance, and the struggle for independence, as well as the challenges and aspirations of modern Zimbabwe.

But amid this historical narrative, one constant thread runs through it all—the enduring spirit of Zimbabwe and its people. It is a spirit that has weathered the storms of time, and like the ancient stone walls of Great Zimbabwe, it stands strong, a testament to the resilience and determination of a nation.

The Origins of Zimbabwe: Early Inhabitants and Cultures

The story of Zimbabwe's origins is a tale that stretches back through millennia, to a time when the land was first inhabited by the earliest peoples of southern Africa. These ancient inhabitants left behind a rich legacy that continues to shape the country's cultural and historical landscape.

Before recorded history, Zimbabwe's landscape was populated by hunter-gatherer communities. These early inhabitants, often referred to as the San or Bushmen, were the first to call this land home. They were nomadic by nature, relying on their intimate knowledge of the environment to gather food, hunt game, and find water sources. The San people are known for their distinctive rock art, which can still be found in various parts of Zimbabwe today, providing glimpses into their way of life and beliefs.

As time passed, the San were joined by other groups of people, such as the Khoikhoi and Bantu-speaking migrants, who brought with them agricultural practices and ironworking skills. The Bantu migrations, which began around 2000 years ago, played a pivotal role in shaping the cultural and linguistic diversity of the region. These migrations brought new crops, technologies, and social structures to the area, contributing to the formation of distinct ethnic groups.

Among the most significant of these ethnic groups were the Shona, who are believed to have migrated to the region around 1000 CE. The Shona people settled in various parts of what is now Zimbabwe and began cultivating crops such as millet and sorghum. Over time, they developed complex societies with organized leadership structures and distinct cultural practices.

In the southeastern part of the country, near the border with South Africa, the kingdom of Mapungubwe emerged around the 11th century. This powerful kingdom engaged in trade with the Indian Ocean coast and became known for its impressive artifacts, including goldwork and pottery. The rise of Mapungubwe marked an important phase in the region's history, reflecting its integration into broader networks of trade and cultural exchange.

Another notable civilization of early Zimbabwe was the Khami Kingdom, which succeeded Mapungubwe around the 14th century. The Khami people, like their predecessors, engaged in trade and built stone structures, although on a smaller scale than Great Zimbabwe. Their kingdom thrived for several centuries before succumbing to internal and external pressures.

These early cultures and kingdoms laid the foundation for the development of more advanced societies in Zimbabwe's history, setting the stage for the rise of the Great Zimbabwe civilization, which we will explore in greater detail in later chapters. The interplay of different cultures, migrations, and environmental factors shaped the diverse tapestry of Zimbabwe's early history, a tapestry that continues to be unraveled by archaeologists and historians to this day.

Great Zimbabwe: The Enigmatic Stone City

Great Zimbabwe, an ancient stone city shrouded in mystery and wonder, stands as one of Africa's most remarkable archaeological sites. Located in the southeastern part of present-day Zimbabwe, it is a testament to the architectural and engineering prowess of its builders and the sophistication of the civilization that thrived within its walls.

The origins of Great Zimbabwe date back to around the 11th century, although the exact timeline remains a subject of scholarly debate. This enigmatic city was constructed by the ancestors of the Shona people, who inhabited the region and left behind a legacy that continues to captivate historians, archaeologists, and tourists alike.

At the heart of Great Zimbabwe lies the Great Enclosure, an imposing structure that is a marvel of dry-stone construction. The walls, built without the use of mortar, consist of precisely cut granite blocks that fit together with astonishing precision. Some of these blocks weigh several tons, and the manner in which they were quarried, transported, and assembled remains a subject of ongoing study and fascination.

The Great Enclosure is just one of several stone structures that make up the city. Spread across the complex are other enclosures, walls, and passageways, each with its own unique features and purpose. The Hill Complex, perched on a rocky outcrop, provides a panoramic view of the surrounding landscape and is believed to have served as both a royal residence and a place of ritual significance.

One of the enduring mysteries of Great Zimbabwe is the purpose of the city itself. While it is clear that it was a center of trade, as evidenced by its strategic location along trade routes, the exact nature of its governance, society, and economy continues to be a topic of scholarly inquiry. Some theories suggest that it was a royal city, serving as the capital of a powerful kingdom, while others propose that it was a religious or spiritual center.

The artifacts discovered within Great Zimbabwe offer further insights into its history and culture. Gold, copper, and ivory objects, as well as pottery and glass beads, provide evidence of the city's engagement in long-distance trade with coastal and interior regions. The famous Zimbabwe Bird, a soapstone sculpture with a bird-like shape, is an iconic symbol of the site and its associated civilization.

Over the centuries, Great Zimbabwe faced both periods of growth and decline. Environmental factors, changes in trade routes, and shifts in political power all played a role in its eventual decline. By the 15th century, the city was largely abandoned, and the reasons for its abandonment remain a subject of study and speculation.

Today, Great Zimbabwe stands as a UNESCO World Heritage Site, drawing visitors from around the world who come to marvel at its ancient stone architecture and ponder the mysteries of its past. It serves as a symbol of Zimbabwean heritage and cultural identity, a reminder of the achievements of those who built it, and a testament to the enduring allure of history's enigmas.

Kingdoms of the Past: Mapungubwe and Khami

In the annals of Zimbabwe's rich history, two kingdoms stand as significant precursors to the greatness of Great Zimbabwe itself. The kingdoms of Mapungubwe and Khami, though distinct in their character and achievements, played vital roles in shaping the cultural, economic, and social landscape of ancient Zimbabwe.

Mapungubwe, often referred to as the Kingdom of Mapungubwe, emerged around the 11th century CE in what is now the northern part of Zimbabwe, near the border with South Africa. This kingdom was characterized by its unique social structure and extensive trade networks, making it a vital center of commerce and culture in the region.

At the heart of Mapungubwe was the famous Mapungubwe Hill, an imposing sandstone plateau that served as the royal residence and administrative center of the kingdom. The hill was adorned with palaces, living quarters, and other structures that reflected the societal hierarchy and artistic achievements of the time.

One of the most significant discoveries at Mapungubwe was a wealth of artifacts, including gold objects, pottery, glass beads, and ivory carvings. These items pointed to the kingdom's involvement in long-distance trade with distant regions, including the Indian Ocean coast. The presence of goldwork, in particular, highlighted the prosperity and sophistication of Mapungubwe's society.

The decline of Mapungubwe is still a matter of debate among historians and archaeologists. Environmental factors, such as changes in rainfall patterns and deforestation, have been suggested as contributing factors. Additionally, political shifts and conflicts may have played a role in its ultimate downfall.

Following the decline of Mapungubwe, the region saw the rise of the Khami Kingdom. Khami, located in the southwestern part of Zimbabwe, near the city of Bulawayo, became prominent during the 14th century. While it did not reach the grandeur of Great Zimbabwe, Khami had its own unique characteristics and contributions.

Khami is renowned for its stone architecture, characterized by finely crafted walls made from granite blocks. The city was built on a hillside and featured numerous terraces, enclosures, and platforms. Like Mapungubwe, Khami was involved in trade, with evidence of trade connections with coastal and interior regions.

One of the intriguing aspects of Khami is its relationship with the earlier cultures of the region, including the builders of Great Zimbabwe. Some argue that Khami represented a continuation of architectural and cultural traditions established by these earlier civilizations, while others see it as a distinct and evolving entity.

As with many ancient civilizations, Khami faced its own challenges and eventual decline. Factors such as political instability, environmental changes, and shifts in trade routes likely contributed to its abandonment. The story of Khami serves as a testament to the ebb and flow of history and the interconnectedness of Zimbabwe's past.

Mapungubwe and Khami, though lesser-known than Great Zimbabwe, provide valuable insights into the complexity and diversity of Zimbabwe's history. They stand as reminders of the ingenuity and resilience of the people who inhabited this region, leaving behind a legacy that continues to be explored and celebrated today.

The Rise of the Rozvi Empire

The Rozvi Empire, a formidable and influential kingdom in the pre-colonial history of Zimbabwe, emerged as a dominant power in the 17th century, shaping the political and cultural landscape of the region. Its rise to prominence was marked by a series of complex events and the convergence of various factors.

The roots of the Rozvi Empire can be traced back to the Mutapa Empire, which had exerted significant influence in the region for centuries. However, by the 17th century, the Mutapa Empire had started to weaken due to internal strife, external pressures, and the depletion of resources, leaving a power vacuum that the Rozvi would eventually fill.

The rise of the Rozvi Empire was facilitated by a dynamic leader, Changamire Dombo. Dombo's leadership and strategic prowess were instrumental in the formation of a new centralized kingdom that would later be known as the Rozvi Empire. Under his guidance, the Rozvi capital, known as Danangombe (also referred to as Dhlo-Dhlo or Naletale), was established.

One of the key features of the Rozvi Empire was its formidable military force. The Rozvi warriors, known as the Mambo, were renowned for their skill in battle and their use of innovative tactics. They wielded iron weapons, such as spears and axes, which they produced through ironworking skills acquired from earlier cultures. The Rozvi Empire's territorial expansion was marked by a series of conquests and alliances with neighboring states. It extended its influence over a vast region, encompassing parts of present-day Zimbabwe, Mozambique, and Zambia. The empire controlled crucial trade routes, including those leading to the Indian Ocean coast, which allowed it to amass wealth and resources.

Trade was a significant driver of the Rozvi Empire's prosperity. Gold, ivory, copper, and other valuable commodities were traded both regionally and internationally. The empire's control of these trade networks gave it economic leverage and facilitated the accumulation of wealth.

The religious and cultural practices of the Rozvi Empire were influenced by a combination of indigenous beliefs and external influences. Elements of ancestral worship, divination, and rainmaking played a role in the spiritual life of the empire. The empire's rulers held significant religious authority, and the capital city, Danangombe, had structures and rituals dedicated to religious ceremonies.

As with many historical empires, the Rozvi Empire faced challenges and internal conflicts. Succession disputes, external threats, and the ever-shifting dynamics of power eventually contributed to its decline. The empire's downfall was hastened by the arrival of the Portuguese and other European colonial powers in the region during the late 19th century.

The legacy of the Rozvi Empire endures in the cultural and historical memory of Zimbabwe. It represents a period of innovation, expansion, and complex interactions that shaped the course of regional history. The rise and fall of the Rozvi Empire exemplify the intricate tapestry of Zimbabwe's past, where empires, cultures, and civilizations converged and left indelible marks on the nation's heritage.

The Shona and Ndebele Peoples: Founders of Zimbabwe

The story of Zimbabwe's origins and its rich cultural tapestry is intrinsically tied to the Shona and Ndebele peoples, two prominent ethnic groups that have played pivotal roles in shaping the nation's history and identity.

The Shona, one of the largest ethnic groups in Zimbabwe, have a long and complex history in the region. They are believed to have migrated to what is now Zimbabwe from the north, bringing with them their Bantu language, which is the foundation of many of the country's indigenous languages, including Shona. The Shona settled in various parts of Zimbabwe, adapting to the diverse geographical and ecological landscapes of the region.

These early Shona communities engaged in agriculture, cultivating crops such as millet, sorghum, and maize. They were skilled potters, producing intricate pottery designs that remain a hallmark of Shona artistic expression. Over time, the Shona developed complex societies with organized governance structures and spiritual beliefs that revolved around ancestor worship and connections with the natural world.

One of the most significant contributions of the Shona to Zimbabwe's cultural heritage is their architecture, particularly the construction of stone buildings. The stone city of Great Zimbabwe, which we explored in an earlier chapter, is a testament to their architectural prowess. The Shona people, through generations of craftsmanship, developed the dry-stone construction techniques that allowed them to create impressive structures without the use of mortar.

The Great Zimbabwe city, with its massive stone walls and complex layout, is a striking example of Shona architecture and engineering. It served as a political and economic center and is believed to have been the heart of a Shona kingdom or confederation. The city's design, with its narrow passages and imposing walls, reflects the society's organization and the control exerted by its rulers.

The Ndebele people, on the other hand, have a more recent history in Zimbabwe, dating back to the early 19th century. Their arrival in the region is closely associated with the Mfecane, a period of upheaval and migration in southern Africa. The Ndebele, led by their warrior king Mzilikazi, moved into what is now Zimbabwe after a series of conflicts and migrations.

Mzilikazi's warriors, known as the Ndebele or Matabele, established a formidable military state in the southwestern part of Zimbabwe, with Bulawayo as its capital. The Ndebele kingdom was characterized by its centralized rule, martial culture, and strict social hierarchy. They brought their own language, isiNdebele, which is one of Zimbabwe's official languages.

The Ndebele people, like the Shona, made significant contributions to Zimbabwe's cultural heritage. Their distinctive art forms, including beadwork, architecture, and pottery, reflect their unique identity and artistic expression. The painted homesteads of the Ndebele, adorned with geometric patterns and vibrant colors, are iconic symbols of their culture.

The encounter between the Shona and Ndebele peoples in the 19th century marked a pivotal moment in Zimbabwe's history. It resulted in cultural interactions, conflicts, and the amalgamation of traditions. The Ndebele Kingdom, under King Lobengula, came into contact with the British colonial forces during the late 19th century, leading to the colonization of Zimbabwe.

The Shona and Ndebele peoples remain integral to Zimbabwe's cultural mosaic, contributing to its linguistic, artistic, and spiritual diversity. Their histories are intertwined with the broader narrative of Zimbabwe's past, reflecting the resilience and adaptability of its people in the face of profound historical changes.

The Advent of Arab Traders and Swahili Influence

In the annals of Zimbabwe's history, the arrival of Arab traders and the influence of the Swahili culture mark a significant chapter. This period, which unfolded over centuries, witnessed the convergence of diverse cultures and the exchange of goods, ideas, and knowledge along the intricate web of trade routes that crisscrossed the African continent.

Arab traders first made their presence felt in the Indian Ocean region and along the East African coast as early as the 8th century CE. Over time, their maritime prowess and navigational skills enabled them to establish trade networks that extended to the interior of Africa. Zimbabwe, strategically located in the southern part of the continent, became an integral part of these trade routes.

The Arab traders, primarily from regions such as Oman and the Arabian Peninsula, embarked on long and perilous journeys across the Indian Ocean. They navigated their dhows, traditional sailing vessels, using the monsoon winds that dictated the rhythm of their trade. These skilled navigators and merchants carried a variety of goods, including spices, textiles, porcelain, and precious metals, fostering trade relations that would shape the destiny of the African continent.

One of the key commodities that flowed through these trade networks was gold, extracted from the rich mines of the Zimbabwean interior. Gold was highly prized in the markets of the Middle East and Asia, and the demand for this precious metal fueled the expansion of trade routes into the heart of Africa. Ivory, another sought-after commodity, was also traded extensively, highlighting the region's diverse natural resources.

The arrival of Arab traders in Zimbabwe had a profound impact on the local societies. It introduced new elements, including the Islamic faith and Arabic script, into the cultural mosaic of the region. Arab traders established settlements along the coast, which served as trading posts and centers of cultural exchange.

The Swahili people, who inhabited the East African coast and were influenced by Arab traders, played a significant role in facilitating this exchange. The Swahili culture, characterized by its blend of indigenous African, Arab, and Persian elements, became a bridge connecting the Arab traders with the inland regions of Zimbabwe.

The Swahili language, a Bantu language influenced by Arabic, served as a lingua franca in trade and cultural interactions. Swahili merchants and traders acted as intermediaries, facilitating communication and commerce between the Arab traders and the indigenous peoples of Zimbabwe.

Beyond trade, the Arab traders and the Swahili culture brought new architectural and artistic influences to Zimbabwe. The distinctive coral rag and limestone architecture, common along the Swahili coast, made its way inland, influencing the design of structures in the region. Additionally, the Swahili artistic tradition, characterized by intricate woodcarvings, jewelry, and textiles, left its mark on Zimbabwean artistry.

The advent of Arab traders and the Swahili influence on Zimbabwe was not without its complexities and challenges. Cultural interactions were often accompanied by tensions, and the spread of Islam, while embraced by some, was met with resistance by others. Nevertheless, this period of exchange and encounter laid the groundwork for the diverse and dynamic cultural tapestry that defines Zimbabwe today.

Monomotapa: Zimbabwe's Medieval Empire

In the heart of southern Africa, during the medieval period, a powerful and enigmatic empire known as Monomotapa rose to prominence, leaving an indelible mark on the history and legacy of Zimbabwe. This empire, often shrouded in legend and mystery, flourished in the region, embodying the sophistication and grandeur of its time.

The origins of Monomotapa can be traced back to the heartland of Zimbabwe, with its center of power situated around the Great Zimbabwe city. The empire's name, Monomotapa, is believed to be derived from the Shona words "Munhu Mutapa," which mean "Ruler of the Lands." This reflects the vast territorial extent and influence wielded by the empire.

Monomotapa reached its zenith during the 14th and 15th centuries, a period when its influence extended over a significant portion of southern Africa, including parts of present-day Zimbabwe, Mozambique, Zambia, and South Africa. The empire's territorial control encompassed a diverse range of ecological zones, from the highlands to the lowlands, granting it access to valuable resources and trade routes.

The heart of Monomotapa was the Great Zimbabwe city, a testament to the architectural prowess and organizational capacity of its builders. The city's imposing stone walls, intricate passageways, and complex layout are enduring symbols of the empire's grandeur. Within its confines, structures were dedicated to both political administration and religious ceremonies, attesting to the interplay of power and spirituality in Monomotapa society. One of the key features of the Great Zimbabwe city is the Great Enclosure, an iconic structure with massive stone walls that evoke a sense of awe and wonder. The purpose of this enclosure remains a subject of debate among historians, with theories ranging from it being a royal residence to a place of religious or ritual significance.

Trade was a cornerstone of Monomotapa's prosperity and influence. The empire controlled vital trade routes, including those that linked the interior of Africa with the Indian Ocean coast. This strategic positioning allowed Monomotapa to engage in long-distance trade with the outside world. Gold, ivory, copper, and other precious commodities flowed through its markets, bringing wealth and cultural exchange to the empire.

The wealth and influence of Monomotapa attracted the attention of European explorers, most notably the Portuguese, who arrived in the region during the late 15th century. The Portuguese sought to establish trade relations with Monomotapa and gain access to its coveted resources. These interactions, however, were marked by tensions and misunderstandings, as the empire's rulers were wary of European encroachment.

Over time, internal challenges, such as political disputes and resource depletion, contributed to the decline of Monomotapa. The empire began to fragment into smaller kingdoms and chiefdoms, losing its once-centralized authority. This fragmentation was exacerbated by external pressures, including incursions by European colonists and neighboring states.

Great Zimbabwe's Architecture and Mysteries

Great Zimbabwe, the iconic stone city that stands as one of Africa's most remarkable archaeological sites, continues to captivate the imagination with its awe-inspiring architecture and enduring mysteries. This enigmatic city, nestled in the southeastern part of present-day Zimbabwe, has been a subject of fascination and scholarly inquiry for generations.

At the heart of Great Zimbabwe's architectural marvels are its massive stone walls, constructed without the use of mortar. These dry-stone walls, made from precisely cut granite blocks, fit together with remarkable precision. Some of these blocks weigh several tons, and the techniques employed by the builders to quarry, transport, and assemble them remain the subject of ongoing study and wonder.

The most iconic structure within Great Zimbabwe is the Great Enclosure, a sprawling complex characterized by its massive stone walls, narrow passageways, and a conical tower that has become emblematic of the site. The purpose of this enclosure continues to be a subject of debate among historians and archaeologists, with theories ranging from it being a royal residence to a place of religious or ritual significance.

Beyond the Great Enclosure, Great Zimbabwe boasts a series of other enclosures, walls, and passageways, each with its unique features and historical significance. The Hill

Complex, perched on a rocky outcrop, offers a panoramic view of the surrounding landscape and is believed to have served as both a royal residence and a place of ritual importance.

The architectural precision and complexity of Great Zimbabwe have led scholars to marvel at the organizational and engineering capabilities of its builders. The manner in which the stones were shaped, transported, and assembled is a testament to the skills and knowledge possessed by the ancient inhabitants of the city. Moreover, the deliberate planning and layout of the city reflect a high degree of social organization and centralized authority.

One of the enduring mysteries of Great Zimbabwe is the purpose of the city itself. While it is clear that it was a center of trade, as evidenced by its strategic location along trade routes, the exact nature of its governance, society, and economy remains a topic of scholarly inquiry. Some theories suggest that it was a royal city, serving as the capital of a powerful kingdom, while others propose that it was a religious or spiritual center.

The artifacts discovered within Great Zimbabwe offer further insights into its history and culture. Gold, copper, and ivory objects, as well as pottery and glass beads, provide evidence of the city's engagement in long-distance trade with coastal and interior regions. The famous Zimbabwe Bird, a soapstone sculpture with a bird-like shape, is an iconic symbol of the site and its associated civilization.

Great Zimbabwe's decline is another mystery that continues to be explored. Environmental factors, such as deforestation and soil depletion, have been suggested as contributing factors, as well as shifts in trade routes and political upheaval. The decline of Great Zimbabwe marked the end of its prominence as a regional power and led to its eventual abandonment.

Trade Routes and Indian Ocean Connections

The history of Zimbabwe is intricately intertwined with a vast network of trade routes and connections that spanned across the Indian Ocean. These ancient trade routes facilitated the exchange of goods, cultures, and ideas between the interior of Africa and distant lands, leaving an indelible mark on the region's history and development.

Trade in southern Africa predates recorded history, with indigenous peoples engaged in the exchange of goods long before the arrival of external traders. However, the advent of Arab traders from the Middle East and Persian Gulf in the early centuries of the Common Era marked a significant turning point in the region's trade dynamics. These skilled navigators and merchants sailed their dhows across the Indian Ocean, linking the ports of the Swahili coast with the interior of Africa.

The Indian Ocean trade routes, often collectively referred to as the Swahili trade network, were a complex web of maritime connections that extended from the east coast of Africa to as far as the Arabian Peninsula, India, and even China. These routes were vital arteries of commerce, facilitating the exchange of a wide array of goods, including spices, textiles, porcelain, and precious metals.

One of the most sought-after commodities in this trade was gold, extracted from the mines of the African interior, including Zimbabwe. Gold was highly prized in the markets of the Middle East and Asia, and its demand played a pivotal role in driving the expansion of trade routes into the heart of Africa. Ivory, another valuable resource, was also extensively traded, highlighting the region's abundant natural wealth.

The Indian Ocean trade routes were more than just conduits for goods; they were conduits for culture and ideas. Arab traders brought with them the Islamic faith and the Arabic script, which left a lasting impact on the societies they encountered. These traders also acted as intermediaries, facilitating cultural exchange between the African interior and the wider world.

One of the key cultural exchanges that occurred along these trade routes was the spread of Islam. While some indigenous peoples adopted the Islamic faith, others incorporated elements of Islamic culture into their own traditions. This blending of cultures and religious practices contributed to the rich and diverse cultural tapestry of the region.

The Swahili people, who inhabited the East African coast, played a pivotal role in mediating these cultural exchanges. Their culture, influenced by a fusion of indigenous African, Arab, and Persian elements, became a bridge connecting the Arab traders with the inland regions of Africa. Swahili merchants and traders, often bilingual in Swahili and Arabic, facilitated communication and commerce between different cultures.

The Indian Ocean trade routes were not without their complexities and challenges. Competition among traders and the ever-present risks of piracy and adverse weather conditions were constant factors. Additionally, the interactions along these routes were marked by a blend of cooperation and conflict, as different cultures and interests intersected.

The arrival of European colonial powers in Africa during the late 15th century introduced new dynamics to the Indian Ocean trade routes. European traders sought to establish their presence and gain access to the riches of Africa, leading to tensions and power struggles along the coasts.

The Arrival of European Explorers

The arrival of European explorers in the lands of southern Africa marked a pivotal moment in the history of the region, bringing profound changes and irrevocably altering the course of its development. These explorers, driven by a thirst for discovery, trade, and imperial ambitions, set sail to the distant shores of Africa, forever connecting the continent with the wider world.

One of the earliest European explorers to venture into the southern African interior was Vasco da Gama, a Portuguese navigator, who, in 1497, sailed around the Cape of Good Hope, opening a sea route to the riches of the Indian Ocean. This maritime achievement, which paved the way for further exploration and trade, set the stage for European interactions with the peoples of the region.

In the subsequent decades, Portuguese explorers and traders established a presence along the eastern coast of Africa, establishing fortified trading posts and colonies. They sought to control the lucrative trade in spices, gold, and other commodities, leading to encounters with local African kingdoms and cultures.

By the early 16th century, Portuguese ships were making regular stops along the coast of present-day Mozambique, establishing a foothold in the region. They encountered the vast and complex network of trade routes that crisscrossed southern Africa, connecting the interior with the Indian Ocean coast. These routes had been used for centuries by indigenous peoples and Arab traders.

One of the key motives driving European exploration was the search for gold. European explorers were drawn by tales of the fabled city of Monomotapa, believed to be a source of immense wealth. The legend of Monomotapa, associated with the Great Zimbabwe ruins, captured the imaginations of many early explorers.

Among these explorers was Francisco Barreto, a Portuguese adventurer who led an expedition into the interior of southern Africa in the late 16th century. His journey took him through present-day Zimbabwe, where he encountered indigenous peoples and witnessed the remnants of the once-mighty Monomotapa Empire. Although his expedition was fraught with challenges, it left a lasting record of his encounters and observations.

In the centuries that followed, European interest in southern Africa continued to grow. Dutch and British explorers and traders ventured into the region, establishing settlements and competing for control of strategic ports and territories. The Dutch East India Company, for instance, established a colony at the Cape of Good Hope in 1652, which would later become a crucial waystation for ships traveling between Europe and the East Indies.

The interactions between European settlers and indigenous African societies were complex and often marked by tensions and conflicts. European powers sought to assert their dominance, leading to power struggles and the imposition of colonial rule. The colonization of Zimbabwe and other parts of southern Africa would follow in subsequent centuries, bringing significant changes to the region's political, social, and economic landscape.

Portuguese in Zimbabwe: A Clash of Cultures

The arrival of Portuguese explorers and traders in Zimbabwe during the 16th century marked a significant chapter in the region's history, characterized by complex interactions, cultural clashes, and the pursuit of wealth and dominance. The Portuguese, driven by the desire for trade and territorial expansion, encountered the diverse indigenous cultures of Zimbabwe, setting the stage for a dynamic and often tumultuous period of history.

The Portuguese presence in Zimbabwe was closely tied to their broader imperial ambitions and their desire to control the lucrative trade routes of the Indian Ocean. They sought to establish a foothold in the region, build alliances with local rulers, and gain access to valuable resources, particularly gold.

One of the earliest Portuguese explorers to venture into Zimbabwe was Francisco Barreto, who led an expedition in the late 16th century. Barreto's journey took him deep into the interior of southern Africa, where he encountered indigenous peoples and the remnants of the once-mighty Monomotapa Empire. His interactions with local rulers and his observations of the African landscape left a lasting record of this early encounter.

The Portuguese were not the only Europeans interested in Zimbabwe; the Dutch and British also explored the region, establishing settlements and competing for control of strategic territories. The Cape of Good Hope, originally a

Dutch colony, became a crucial waystation for ships traveling between Europe and the East Indies, further intensifying European interest in the region.

The encounters between the Portuguese and the indigenous peoples of Zimbabwe were characterized by a clash of cultures. The Portuguese, with their European customs, language, and religious beliefs, often clashed with the deeply rooted traditions and practices of the local African populations.

Religion played a significant role in these interactions. The Portuguese, staunchly Catholic, sought to spread Christianity among the African populations they encountered. They established missions and converted some indigenous peoples to Christianity, while others resisted religious conversion.

Trade was another focal point of contact and conflict. The Portuguese sought to control trade routes and monopolize the lucrative commerce in gold, ivory, and other valuable commodities. This competition for resources and dominance often led to tensions and power struggles with local rulers and rival European powers.

The Portuguese also brought diseases such as smallpox and measles, which had devastating consequences for the indigenous populations. The introduction of firearms by the Portuguese into local conflicts further disrupted the balance of power in the region.

As European influence expanded, the dynamics of southern Africa were fundamentally transformed. The colonization of Zimbabwe and other parts of southern Africa by European powers in the centuries that followed had far-reaching consequences, including changes in governance, land ownership, and social structures. These changes shaped the course of Zimbabwean history, setting the stage for the complex challenges and opportunities that the nation would face in the modern era.

Mutapa Empire: The Golden Age

The Mutapa Empire, also known as the Monomotapa Empire, stands as one of the most influential and enduring empires in the history of southern Africa. Its golden age, spanning several centuries, was marked by remarkable achievements in governance, trade, and culture, leaving an indelible legacy that continues to shape the history of the region.

The origins of the Mutapa Empire can be traced back to the heartland of southern Africa, with its center of power situated near the confluence of the Zambezi and Limpopo Rivers, an area that encompasses present-day Zimbabwe. The empire's name, "Mutapa" or "Monomotapa," has been linked to the Shona words "Munhu Mutapa," meaning "Ruler of the Lands," reflecting the vast territorial extent and influence wielded by the empire.

The Mutapa Empire reached its zenith during the 15th and 16th centuries, a period characterized by remarkable political stability and economic prosperity. Under the leadership of powerful rulers, known as Mutapa, the empire expanded its influence over a vast region, encompassing parts of present-day Zimbabwe, Mozambique, Zambia, and South Africa.

The heart of the Mutapa Empire was the Great Zimbabwe city, an architectural marvel and symbol of its grandeur. While the exact relationship between Great Zimbabwe and the Mutapa Empire remains a subject of scholarly debate, it is clear that Great Zimbabwe played a significant role in the empire's political and cultural life.

One of the key achievements of the Mutapa Empire was its organization and governance. The empire was characterized by a centralized authority, with the Mutapa at its helm. Below the Mutapa were a hierarchy of officials, including provincial governors and local chiefs, who helped administer the empire's vast territories. This governance structure ensured the empire's stability and efficient administration.

Trade was a cornerstone of the Mutapa Empire's prosperity and influence. The empire controlled vital trade routes, including those leading to the Indian Ocean coast. This strategic positioning allowed it to engage in long-distance trade with the outside world. Gold, ivory, copper, and other precious commodities flowed through its markets, bringing wealth and cultural exchange to the empire.

The trade networks of the Mutapa Empire extended as far as the Indian Ocean, facilitating exchanges with the Swahili coast and beyond. These connections brought a wealth of goods, including spices, textiles, and porcelain, into the empire. The city of Sofala, a major port on the Indian Ocean coast, served as a crucial hub in this trade network.

The prosperity of the Mutapa Empire attracted the attention of European explorers, particularly the Portuguese, who arrived in the region during the late 15th century. The Portuguese sought to establish trade relations with the Mutapa and gain access to its coveted resources, particularly gold. These interactions, however, were marked by tensions and misunderstandings, as the Mutapa rulers were wary of European encroachment.

The Mutapa Empire also left a rich cultural legacy. It played a significant role in the development of the Shona language and culture, which endure in Zimbabwe to this day. The empire's rulers held both political and religious authority, and they presided over rituals and ceremonies that connected them to the spiritual realm.

Over time, internal challenges, such as political disputes and resource depletion, contributed to the decline of the Mutapa Empire. External pressures, including conflicts with neighboring states and the arrival of European colonial powers, hastened its downfall.

The legacy of the Mutapa Empire endures in the cultural and historical memory of Zimbabwe and southern Africa. It represents a period of political sophistication, architectural innovation, and economic prosperity. The rise and fall of the Mutapa Empire exemplify the complex tapestry of African history, where empires, cultures, and civilizations converged and left indelible marks on the region's heritage.

The Impact of the Transatlantic Slave Trade

The Transatlantic Slave Trade, one of the darkest chapters in human history, had a profound and lasting impact on Africa, the Americas, and Europe. This vast and brutal system of forced labor and human trafficking, spanning over four centuries, left a legacy that continues to shape societies and economies to this day.

The origins of the Transatlantic Slave Trade can be traced back to the early 16th century when European powers, including Portugal, Spain, England, France, and the Netherlands, established colonies in the Americas. These colonies required a vast labor force to cultivate crops such as sugar, tobacco, and cotton, which were in high demand in Europe.

The demand for labor led to the systematic abduction and enslavement of millions of Africans. Slavery was not a new institution in Africa, but the scale and brutality of the Transatlantic Slave Trade were unprecedented. African kingdoms and tribes were drawn into this trade, either as willing participants or through coercion and violence.

The process of enslavement was dehumanizing and brutal. Africans were captured through raids, wars, or by local African rulers who profited from the trade. They were often subjected to grueling forced marches to the coast, where they would be held in coastal forts and dungeons under horrific conditions.

Once on the ships, known as slave vessels or "floating coffins," Africans endured unimaginable suffering. The Middle Passage, the harrowing journey across the Atlantic Ocean, was marked by overcrowding, disease, malnutrition, and extreme cruelty. Countless Africans died during this passage, their bodies cast overboard.

Those who survived the Middle Passage faced a life of unrelenting hardship in the Americas. They were subjected to forced labor on plantations and in mines, enduring brutal working conditions, physical abuse, and deplorable living conditions. Families were torn apart, and African cultures were suppressed in a relentless effort to strip slaves of their identities.

The impact of the Transatlantic Slave Trade on Africa was devastating. Entire regions were depopulated, with millions of people forcibly removed from their homelands. The social fabric of African societies was torn apart, as families and communities were shattered. The loss of able-bodied individuals had profound economic consequences for African societies.

The trade also perpetuated instability and conflict in Africa. Rival African groups often competed to capture slaves and trade them with European powers, leading to violence and upheaval. The slave trade contributed to the erosion of traditional African political systems and the rise of new power structures centered around the trade in human beings.

In the Americas, the impact of the Transatlantic Slave Trade was equally profound. African labor was the backbone of the colonial and early American economies, contributing to the wealth of European powers and the development of the New World. Slavery became deeply ingrained in the social and economic fabric of the Americas.

The legacy of slavery in the Americas is still felt today, with deep-seated racial inequalities and disparities persisting. Slavery left an indelible mark on the cultural, social, and political landscape of the Americas, shaping issues of race, identity, and civil rights.

In Europe, the Transatlantic Slave Trade fueled economic growth and the rise of global empires. The profits from the trade enriched European nations and financed further exploration and colonization. However, it also raised moral and ethical questions, leading to debates and movements against the institution of slavery.

Abolitionist movements gained momentum in the late 18th and 19th centuries, leading to the eventual abolition of the Transatlantic Slave Trade and slavery itself in many parts of the Americas and Europe. The struggle for freedom and equality by enslaved Africans and their descendants, such as the Haitian Revolution and the American Civil Rights Movement, played crucial roles in these transformations.

The legacy of the Transatlantic Slave Trade continues to shape contemporary debates on race, reparations, and social justice. It serves as a stark reminder of the depths of human cruelty and suffering, as well as the resilience and strength of those who resisted and persevered. The impact of this tragic chapter in history reverberates through the generations, reminding us of the importance of acknowledging and confronting the enduring legacies of slavery.

The Scramble for Africa: British and Rhodesia

The late 19th century witnessed a frenzied period of imperial expansion and colonization in Africa known as the "Scramble for Africa." European powers, driven by economic interests, geopolitical rivalries, and a desire to assert control over new territories, embarked on a race to claim and dominate vast swaths of the African continent. Among the European powers involved, the British Empire played a prominent role in the colonization of Africa, and the region that would become known as Rhodesia became a significant part of this colonial enterprise.

The scramble for Africa was spurred by a confluence of factors, including the industrial revolution in Europe, which increased the demand for raw materials, the need for new markets for European goods, and a desire to secure strategic trade routes and geopolitical advantages. It was in this context that European powers sought to expand their colonial holdings in Africa.

The British Empire, one of the most formidable colonial powers of the era, had established a presence along the coastlines of Africa through its African trading companies, missionary activities, and naval power. However, the interior of the continent remained largely uncharted and unclaimed. This changed with the advent of European explorers, such as David Livingstone and Henry Morton Stanley, who ventured into the heart of Africa and sparked European interest in its interior.

The British sought to secure control over key regions and trade routes in Africa. Cecil Rhodes, a British imperialist and businessman, played a pivotal role in British expansion in southern Africa. He was instrumental in the formation of the British South Africa Company (BSAC), which obtained a royal charter in 1889, granting it rights to administer and colonize vast territories in southern Africa.

Rhodesia, named after Cecil Rhodes, emerged as a central focus of British colonial ambitions. It encompassed the areas of present-day Zimbabwe and Zambia. The BSAC established administrative authority over this region, with the aim of exploiting its mineral resources, particularly gold and diamonds. This marked the beginning of the colonization of Rhodesia.

The colonization of Rhodesia was marked by the imposition of British colonial rule and the dispossession of indigenous African populations from their ancestral lands. The British authorities sought to establish control over the territory, introduce European settlers, and exploit its natural resources for the benefit of the British Empire.

The indigenous peoples of Rhodesia, primarily the Shona and Ndebele, resisted British encroachment and colonial rule. The First Chimurenga (1896-1897) and the Second Chimurenga (1964-1979) were armed uprisings against colonial rule, led by African leaders such as Mbuya Nehanda, Sekuru Kaguvi, and later figures like Joshua Nkomo and Robert Mugabe. These movements were characterized by fierce resistance and the assertion of African identity and rights.

The British government eventually established direct colonial rule over Rhodesia, leading to the formation of

Southern Rhodesia and Northern Rhodesia (present-day Zambia). Southern Rhodesia became a self-governing British colony in 1923, with a predominantly white settler population that controlled political and economic power.

The colonial period in Rhodesia was marked by racial segregation, discrimination, and the suppression of African political aspirations. The policies of apartheid-like segregation and disenfranchisement of the African majority created deep social divisions and tensions.

The struggle for independence in Rhodesia was protracted and marked by both armed and diplomatic efforts. In 1965, the white minority government, led by Ian Smith, unilaterally declared independence from Britain, resulting in international isolation and sanctions. The armed struggle continued, led by groups like the Zimbabwe African National Liberation Army (ZANLA) and the Zimbabwe People's Revolutionary Army (ZIPRA).

In 1980, after years of negotiations and a Lancaster House Agreement, Rhodesia gained independence as the Republic of Zimbabwe. Robert Mugabe became the first Prime Minister, and later President, of the newly independent nation. Zimbabwe's journey from colonialism to independence was a complex and tumultuous one, marked by both hope and challenges.

Colonial Rule and the Land Question

Colonial rule in Zimbabwe, as in many parts of Africa, brought profound changes to the land and its ownership. The question of land, its distribution, and its impact on the indigenous population became a central issue during the colonial period and continues to shape the nation's history and politics.

When the British South Africa Company (BSAC) and Cecil Rhodes' imperial ambitions led to the colonization of Zimbabwe, the indigenous African population's relationship with the land underwent a seismic shift. Prior to colonization, land ownership and usage in Zimbabwe were largely communal, with different ethnic groups, such as the Shona and Ndebele, practicing subsistence agriculture and animal husbandry.

The British colonial authorities introduced the notion of private property and land tenure, a concept that was foreign to the traditional African societies. Land was classified into commercial farms, European-owned land, and communal land, with the latter allocated to indigenous African communities.

The Land Apportionment Act of 1930 further institutionalized racial segregation and land allocation. It divided land into distinct racial zones, with the majority of arable land reserved for white settlers. The indigenous African population was confined to overcrowded and often infertile reserves.

This system of land allocation created stark disparities in landownership and access to resources. White settlers, who constituted a small minority of the population, controlled the most fertile and productive land, while indigenous Africans were relegated to less arable areas. This racialized land distribution became a source of deep-seated inequality and resentment.

The impact of colonial land policies extended beyond economic disparities. The dispossession of indigenous Africans from their ancestral lands disrupted social and cultural norms. Communities were uprooted, and their traditional ways of life were profoundly altered. The sense of belonging to the land and the cultural significance of territory were deeply affected.

The colonial period also witnessed the transformation of agriculture in Zimbabwe. The large commercial farms owned by white settlers became the primary engines of agricultural production, specializing in cash crops such as tobacco, maize, and cotton. Indigenous African communities, confined to reserves, often practiced subsistence agriculture on marginal lands.

The legacy of colonial land policies looms large in the history of Zimbabwe. The disparities in landownership and access to resources created during this period would become central issues in the struggle for independence and post-colonial governance.

The Land Tenure Act of 1969, which sought to address some of the inequalities in land ownership, fell short of meeting the aspirations of the African majority. Land redistribution efforts during the early years of independence faced challenges, including resistance from some white farmers and international pressures.

The fast-track land reform program initiated in the early 2000s, under President Robert Mugabe's leadership, aimed to accelerate land redistribution to address historical injustices. This program, characterized by land seizures and resettlement of black farmers, resulted in significant changes in land ownership and use. It also sparked controversy, economic disruptions, and international repercussions.

The land question in Zimbabwe remains a complex and contentious issue. It is central to debates about economic development, social justice, and political stability in the country. The challenges of reconciling historical injustices with the need for agricultural productivity and sustainable land use continue to shape Zimbabwe's political landscape and future.

Struggles for Independence: Chimurenga Wars

The quest for independence in Zimbabwe, marked by a series of armed uprisings known as the Chimurenga wars, was a pivotal and tumultuous period in the nation's history. These protracted and often brutal conflicts were driven by the desire to end colonial rule, achieve self-determination, and redress historical injustices.

The First Chimurenga, also known as the First Chimurenga War or the First Zimbabwean War of Independence, erupted between 1896 and 1897. It was a widespread armed rebellion against British colonial rule, characterized by fierce resistance from indigenous African communities. The term "Chimurenga" itself is derived from the Shona word meaning "struggle" or "revolution."

The immediate causes of the First Chimurenga were rooted in the oppressive conditions imposed by colonial rule. The indigenous African population endured forced labor, land dispossession, and racial discrimination. Additionally, the imposition of colonial taxes and the alienation of their ancestral lands fueled discontent and resistance.

The First Chimurenga was not a coordinated or centralized movement but rather a series of localized uprisings led by different African leaders and communities. Prominent figures such as Mbuya Nehanda, Sekuru Kaguvi, and Kaguvi's wife, Nyakasikana, played pivotal roles in mobilizing resistance.

The uprisings spread across the country, with battles and skirmishes occurring in various regions. The indigenous fighters employed a range of tactics, including guerrilla warfare and spiritual symbolism. Mbuya Nehanda, in particular, became a symbol of resistance and defiance.

The British colonial authorities responded to the uprisings with a brutal crackdown. Indigenous fighters faced superior firepower, and the conflict resulted in significant loss of life on both sides. British forces employed scorched-earth tactics, burning villages and crops to deprive the rebels of support.

The First Chimurenga ultimately ended in defeat for the indigenous African population. The resistance was fragmented and lacked the organizational cohesion to withstand the British colonial forces. Many African leaders were captured, tried, and executed, while others went into hiding.

Despite its ultimate failure, the First Chimurenga laid the groundwork for future struggles for independence. It galvanized a sense of national identity and resistance against colonial oppression. The memory of Mbuya Nehanda and other leaders who had sacrificed their lives for the cause of freedom became enduring symbols of Zimbabwean nationalism.

The Second Chimurenga, also known as the Second Chimurenga War or the Rhodesian Bush War, unfolded from the 1960s to 1979 and represented a more coordinated and sustained effort to achieve independence from the white minority government of Rhodesia.

The Second Chimurenga was marked by the emergence of organized liberation movements, notably the Zimbabwe African National Union (ZANU) and the Zimbabwe African People's Union (ZAPU). These movements, led by figures like Robert Mugabe, Joshua Nkomo, and Herbert Chitepo, sought to unite the fragmented resistance and wage a more strategic struggle against colonial rule.

The armed conflict intensified throughout the 1970s. Guerrilla fighters launched attacks against Rhodesian security forces and infrastructure, while political efforts, including international diplomacy and negotiations, also played a role in pressuring the Rhodesian government to the negotiating table.

The Lancaster House Agreement, brokered by the British government in 1979, paved the way for a ceasefire and a transition to majority rule. Zimbabwe achieved independence on April 18, 1980, with Robert Mugabe becoming the nation's first Prime Minister.

The legacy of the Chimurenga wars looms large in Zimbabwe's history and national identity. The struggles for independence, marked by courage, sacrifice, and determination, led to the end of colonial rule and the birth of a new nation. However, the post-independence era brought its own set of challenges and complexities, as Zimbabwe grappled with issues of governance, land reform, and economic development. The memory of the Chimurenga wars remains a potent symbol of the country's resilience and its ongoing journey toward a more just and equitable future.

Robert Mugabe and the Birth of Modern Zimbabwe

Robert Gabriel Mugabe, a towering figure in the history of Zimbabwe and African politics, played a central role in the birth of modern Zimbabwe. His leadership, from the early years of independence until his resignation in 2017, shaped the nation's trajectory, leaving an indelible mark on its political, social, and economic landscape.

Born on February 21, 1924, in what was then Southern Rhodesia, Robert Mugabe came of age during a time of colonial oppression and racial segregation. He pursued his education with determination, attending mission schools and later studying in South Africa and Ghana, where he was influenced by the ideals of African nationalism and liberation.

Mugabe's early political activism emerged in the 1960s when he became involved in the struggle against white minority rule in Rhodesia. He was a key figure in the Zimbabwe African National Union (ZANU), one of the liberation movements fighting for independence. His political acumen and commitment to the cause earned him recognition among both supporters and adversaries.

The Second Chimurenga, or Rhodesian Bush War, was a pivotal moment in Mugabe's political career. ZANU, led by Mugabe, waged a guerrilla campaign against the white minority government of Ian Smith. The war, characterized by fierce battles and negotiations, ultimately led to the

Lancaster House Agreement in 1979, which paved the way for Zimbabwe's independence in 1980.

Following independence, Robert Mugabe became the country's first Prime Minister. His leadership was initially characterized by efforts to bridge racial divides and promote reconciliation. The new nation faced immense challenges, including land ownership disparities, a fragile economy, and the need to establish a functional government.

Mugabe's early years in power garnered international acclaim for his conciliatory stance and commitment to nation-building. However, it wasn't long before political tensions and complex issues began to emerge. One of the most significant challenges was the issue of land reform.

Land reform had been a longstanding grievance dating back to colonial times. The majority of fertile land in Zimbabwe was owned by a small white minority, while the indigenous African population was relegated to overcrowded reserves. Mugabe's government faced growing pressure to address this issue and redistribute land more equitably.

In the late 1990s and early 2000s, Zimbabwe experienced a tumultuous period marked by controversial land seizures and economic instability. The fast-track land reform program, initiated by Mugabe's government, aimed to accelerate land redistribution to black farmers but was marred by violence, disruptions in agricultural production, and international condemnation.

This period also saw political challenges, including contested elections and allegations of human rights abuses. Mugabe's presidency faced criticism from both domestic and international quarters for its handling of political opposition and its governance record.

Despite these challenges, Mugabe remained a dominant figure in Zimbabwean politics for several decades. He consolidated power within his party, the Zimbabwe African National Union-Patriotic Front (ZANU-PF), and won multiple presidential elections, albeit amidst controversy and accusations of electoral misconduct.

Mugabe's leadership style evolved over time, from the early years of reconciliation to a more authoritarian and divisive approach in later years. His government's policies, including land reform and indigenization initiatives, had a profound impact on the country's economy and political landscape.

In November 2017, facing increasing pressure and a military intervention, Robert Mugabe resigned as President of Zimbabwe after nearly 37 years in power. His departure marked the end of an era and signaled a new chapter in the country's history.

The legacy of Robert Mugabe remains deeply complex and polarizing. He is celebrated by some as a liberation hero who fought against colonialism and apartheid-era South Africa. Others view his later years in power as marked by authoritarianism, economic mismanagement, and human rights abuses.

The Legacy of Liberation Movements

The legacy of liberation movements in Africa is a complex tapestry woven from the struggles for independence, the pursuit of self-determination, and the promise of a better future. These movements emerged in the mid-20th century as African nations sought to break free from the shackles of colonialism, imperialism, and racial oppression. Their impact on the continent, both during the struggle for independence and in the post-independence era, has been profound and multifaceted.

The origins of liberation movements in Africa can be traced to the colonial period, when African nations were subjected to foreign rule and exploitation. European powers, including Britain, France, Belgium, and Portugal, established colonies across the continent, imposing their authority and extracting valuable resources. The African population faced discrimination, land dispossession, and economic exploitation, sparking discontent and resistance.

The desire for self-determination and the quest for independence became driving forces behind the formation of liberation movements. These movements took various forms and were led by charismatic figures who inspired hope and unity among their people. Prominent leaders such as Kwame Nkrumah of Ghana, Jomo Kenyatta of Kenya, and Julius Nyerere of Tanzania emerged as iconic figures in the struggle for independence.

The methods employed by liberation movements were diverse, ranging from peaceful protests and diplomatic negotiations to armed resistance and guerrilla warfare. The intensity of the struggle varied from one nation to another, reflecting the unique historical, social, and political contexts of each country.

One of the most iconic and successful liberation movements in Africa was the African National Congress (ANC) in South Africa. Led by figures like Nelson Mandela, Oliver Tambo, and Walter Sisulu, the ANC waged a protracted struggle against apartheid, a system of racial segregation and discrimination. The organization's resilience and global support eventually led to the dismantling of apartheid and the inauguration of Nelson Mandela as South Africa's first black president in 1994.

In Zimbabwe, the Zimbabwe African National Union (ZANU) and the Zimbabwe African People's Union (ZAPU), led by figures like Robert Mugabe and Joshua Nkomo, played pivotal roles in the struggle against white minority rule. The Second Chimurenga, or Rhodesian Bush War, ultimately led to the Lancaster House Agreement in 1979 and Zimbabwe's independence in 1980.

Liberation movements in other African nations, including Angola, Mozambique, Namibia, and Eritrea, also achieved independence through armed struggle and diplomacy. Their struggles were marked by sacrifices, solidarity, and a shared vision of a free and self-determined Africa.

The legacy of liberation movements extends beyond the achievement of independence. These movements, once in power, faced the daunting task of nation-building, reconstruction, and governance. The post-independence era brought both opportunities and challenges as nations grappled with issues such as economic development, political stability, and social justice.

In some cases, liberation movements successfully transitioned into political parties and played key roles in shaping the political landscape of newly independent nations. However, challenges such as corruption, one-party rule, and human rights abuses also marred the record of some liberation movements in power.

The legacy of liberation movements is a mixed one, characterized by both achievements and shortcomings. They brought an end to colonial rule, expanded access to education and healthcare, and promoted national pride and identity. However, they also faced criticism for authoritarianism, economic mismanagement, and political instability.

The enduring impact of liberation movements in Africa can be seen in the ongoing struggles for democracy, good governance, and social justice on the continent. The ideals of freedom, equality, and self-determination continue to inspire African nations as they navigate the complexities of the 21st century.

Wildlife and Conservation in Zimbabwe

Zimbabwe, often referred to as the "Pearl of Africa" for its incredible biodiversity, boasts a rich and diverse tapestry of wildlife and natural landscapes. From vast savannas and lush forests to rugged mountains and meandering rivers, the country's diverse ecosystems provide a habitat for an astonishing array of species, making it a haven for wildlife enthusiasts and conservationists alike.

One of the most iconic and majestic animals found in Zimbabwe is the African elephant. These gentle giants roam freely in the country's national parks and wildlife reserves, including Hwange National Park, which is home to one of Africa's largest elephant populations. The sight of a herd of elephants, with their lumbering grace, is a common and awe-inspiring experience for visitors.

Zimbabwe is also renowned for its populations of other "Big Five" species, including the African lion, African leopard, African buffalo, and white rhinoceros. These charismatic animals are the stars of safari adventures in the country, drawing tourists from around the world. Conservation efforts have been instrumental in protecting these species and their habitats.

Hwange National Park, covering over 14,600 square kilometers, is not only a haven for elephants but also offers refuge to a diverse range of wildlife, including giraffes, zebras, cheetahs, and numerous antelope species. The park's varied landscapes, from grassy plains to mopane woodlands, provide vital habitats for these creatures.

Lake Kariba, the world's largest human-made reservoir, is another vital wildlife habitat. The lake and its surrounding area are home to numerous bird species, including fish eagles, herons, and cormorants. It's also a hotspot for Nile crocodiles and hippos.

Zimbabwe's vast wilderness areas are a testament to its commitment to conservation. The nation has established numerous national parks, wildlife reserves, and protected areas to safeguard its natural heritage. These protected spaces not only serve as refuges for wildlife but also offer visitors a chance to witness these animals in their natural habitats.

Mana Pools National Park, a UNESCO World Heritage Site, is famous for its unique walking safaris, allowing visitors to get up close to animals like elephants and lions while on foot. The park is known for its scenic beauty, with the Zambezi River meandering through its floodplains.

Victoria Falls, one of the most renowned natural wonders of the world, is a testament to Zimbabwe's commitment to preserving its natural treasures. The surrounding Zambezi National Park and the Mosi-oa-Tunya National Park in Zambia are dedicated to protecting the ecosystems around this spectacular waterfall.

Conservation efforts in Zimbabwe are not limited to terrestrial ecosystems. The country's waters, including the Zambezi River, are home to diverse fish species, including the iconic tigerfish. These water bodies also support the famous annual migration of the barbel catfish.

The management of these protected areas and the conservation of wildlife in Zimbabwe are significant undertakings that require careful planning, resources, and international cooperation. Zimbabwe has faced challenges such as poaching, habitat loss, and human-wildlife conflicts, but it remains committed to preserving its natural heritage for future generations.

Efforts to combat poaching and protect endangered species, such as the black rhinoceros and African wild dog, have been central to Zimbabwe's conservation initiatives. Conservation organizations, governmental agencies, and local communities collaborate to ensure the survival of these species.

Zimbabwe's commitment to conservation extends beyond its borders. The country actively participates in international conservation efforts and agreements, recognizing that the challenges facing its wildlife are often transnational in nature. Collaboration with neighboring countries and organizations like the Convention on International Trade in Endangered Species of Wild Fauna and Flora (CITES) is integral to safeguarding the nation's biodiversity.

In conclusion, Zimbabwe's wildlife and conservation efforts are integral to the nation's identity and future. The country's diverse ecosystems and iconic species make it a global hotspot for nature enthusiasts and conservationists alike. The legacy of preservation and the commitment to coexisting with wildlife reflect Zimbabwe's dedication to protecting its natural heritage while fostering sustainable tourism and environmental stewardship.

Savory Delights: Zimbabwean Cuisine

Zimbabwean cuisine is a reflection of the country's diverse cultural heritage, with flavors and dishes that showcase a blend of indigenous African, British colonial, and regional influences. From hearty stews to delicious snacks, Zimbabwe offers a tantalizing array of culinary delights that captivate the senses and celebrate its rich history.

One of the staple foods in Zimbabwe is sadza, also known as pap or nsima in other African regions. Sadza is a thick porridge made from maize meal and water. It serves as the foundation of many Zimbabwean meals and is often served alongside a variety of meat, vegetable, and legume dishes. Sadza is typically eaten with the hands, rolled into a ball, and used to scoop up accompanying dishes.

Meat plays a prominent role in Zimbabwean cuisine, with beef, chicken, and goat being popular choices. Nyama, or meat, is often prepared in savory stews and grilled over open flames. Dishes like nyama ne nyadzi (meat and vegetable stew) and braaivleis (barbecue) are beloved by locals and visitors alike.

A signature dish in Zimbabwe is mazondo, a flavorful preparation of beef or goat trotters and knuckles. These meaty morsels are slow-cooked to tender perfection, often accompanied by a rich and spicy gravy. Mazondo is a dish that highlights the resourcefulness of Zimbabwean cooks, making use of every part of the animal.

Another beloved meat dish is biltong, a dried and cured meat snack similar to beef jerky. Biltong can be found throughout Zimbabwe and is a popular choice for a quick and savory treat. It's typically made from beef, but other meats like game animals are also used.

Zimbabwean cuisine also incorporates a wide variety of vegetables and legumes, with leafy greens like collard greens (known as rape) being a common side dish. Pumpkin leaves, also known as muboora, are often cooked with groundnut sauce to create a flavorful and nutritious accompaniment to sadza.

A unique and traditional Zimbabwean specialty is mukimo, a dish made from mashed vegetables such as maize, pumpkin, and potatoes. These ingredients are combined with other seasonings and served as a hearty and satisfying meal.

Zimbabwean cuisine reflects the influence of neighboring countries, particularly South Africa and Zambia. Dishes like boerewors, a flavorful sausage, and chibuku, a locally brewed beer, are enjoyed by many Zimbabweans.

The country's desserts and sweets are simple yet delicious. Maheu is a popular drink made from fermented maize and sugar, offering a sweet and slightly tangy flavor. It's often enjoyed as a refreshing beverage.

Zimbabweans also have a sweet tooth, and you can find treats like mandazi, a type of fried doughnut, and maputi, which are roasted or popped maize kernels often coated in sugar or spices.

When it comes to celebrating special occasions, Zimbabweans have their own unique dishes. For weddings and festivals, dishes like rice with chicken or beef stew, along with vegetables and sadza, are commonly served to guests.

In recent years, Zimbabwean cuisine has been gaining recognition on the international culinary scene. Restaurants in major cities like Harare and Bulawayo offer a diverse range of dishes, from traditional favorites to modern interpretations of classic recipes.

Zimbabwean cuisine is a testament to the country's rich cultural heritage and culinary traditions. It's a cuisine that brings people together, offering flavors that are both comforting and exciting, and inviting everyone to savor the delicious delights that this nation has to offer. Whether enjoying a home-cooked meal with locals or dining at a restaurant, exploring Zimbabwean cuisine is a culinary adventure that leaves a lasting impression.

Victoria Falls: Nature's Grand Spectacle

Victoria Falls, one of the world's most awe-inspiring natural wonders, stands as a testament to the grandeur and beauty of the natural world. Known as "Mosi-oa-Tunya" in the local Tonga language, which means "The Smoke That Thunders," this remarkable waterfall is a majestic manifestation of the power of water and the forces of nature.

Located on the border between Zimbabwe and Zambia, Victoria Falls is a UNESCO World Heritage Site and a must-visit destination for travelers from around the globe. It is often hailed as one of the Seven Natural Wonders of the World, and for good reason.

The falls are formed by the mighty Zambezi River, one of Africa's longest rivers, as it plunges dramatically into a chasm that spans approximately 1,700 meters (5,600 feet) in width and drops to depths of up to 108 meters (354 feet). The result is a spectacle of cascading water that creates a thunderous roar and a mist that can be seen and felt from miles away.

One of the most captivating aspects of Victoria Falls is the sheer volume of water that flows over its precipice, especially during the rainy season. The Zambezi River, swollen with the rains, reaches its peak flow between February and May, causing the falls to become a roaring torrent of water. The mist generated during this period is so thick that it can obscure the falls from view, creating an otherworldly experience for visitors.

The mist from Victoria Falls, often referred to as "the smoke," rises high into the sky and can be visible from a distance of nearly 50 kilometers (30 miles). This phenomenon gave rise to the local Tonga name "Mosi-oa-Tunya" and the English name "The Smoke That Thunders." The constant spray also nourishes the lush rainforest that surrounds the falls, creating a unique microclimate and providing a habitat for a variety of plant and animal species.

One of the most iconic vantage points for viewing Victoria Falls is the aptly named Knife-Edge Bridge, which extends over the gorge and offers a thrilling close-up experience of the cascading waters. Another popular viewpoint is Devil's Pool, a natural rock pool located on the edge of the falls on the Zambian side. Adventurous visitors can swim at the very precipice of the falls during the dry season, providing an adrenaline-pumping encounter with the majestic waters.

While Victoria Falls is a sight to behold year-round, each season offers a different experience. During the dry season, which typically occurs from September to November, the water flow decreases, revealing more of the underlying rock formations. This is an ideal time for photographers to capture the intricate details of the falls.

Beyond its visual grandeur, Victoria Falls offers a range of activities for visitors to explore its natural beauty and surrounding environment. Helicopter and microlight flights provide breathtaking aerial views of the falls and the meandering Zambezi River. Guided walking tours take visitors through the rainforest, where they can witness the unique flora and fauna that thrive in the misty environment.

For the adventurous, white-water rafting on the Zambezi River offers an exhilarating experience with its world-class rapids, and bungee jumping from the Victoria Falls Bridge provides an adrenaline rush like no other.

Victoria Falls is not only a natural wonder but also a symbol of cooperation and shared heritage between Zimbabwe and Zambia. The falls are accessible from both sides, with Victoria Falls Town in Zimbabwe and Livingstone in Zambia serving as the primary entry points. Visitors can easily cross the border to experience the falls from different angles and perspectives.

The cultural significance of Victoria Falls extends beyond its stunning beauty. The indigenous people of the region, particularly the Tonga and Lozi tribes, have long revered the falls as a sacred site. Local traditions and rituals associated with the falls continue to be an integral part of the cultural heritage of the area.

In conclusion, Victoria Falls stands as a testament to the splendor and power of nature. Its breathtaking beauty, thundering waters, and surrounding rainforest create an enchanting and immersive experience for all who have the privilege of witnessing it. This remarkable natural wonder continues to captivate the hearts and minds of people from all corners of the world, inspiring awe and reverence for the majesty of the natural world.

Matobo Hills: Ancient Rock Art and History

Nestled in the heart of Zimbabwe, the Matobo Hills is a place of remarkable beauty, cultural significance, and historical importance. This UNESCO World Heritage Site is a landscape of immense geological and archaeological value, offering a window into the distant past of this captivating region.

The Matobo Hills, also known as the Matopos, are a range of granite hills and kopjes that stretch over approximately 3,100 square kilometers (1,200 square miles) in southern Zimbabwe. These massive granite formations, characterized by their rounded and weathered shapes, create a dramatic and otherworldly landscape that has drawn the admiration of both nature enthusiasts and explorers for centuries.

One of the most intriguing aspects of the Matobo Hills is its rich history, dating back thousands of years. These hills have been inhabited by various indigenous communities, including the San (Bushmen) and later the Ndebele people. Evidence of human habitation, rock paintings, and archaeological sites provide insights into the lives of these ancient cultures.

The San people, who are renowned for their rock art, left a significant cultural legacy in the Matobo Hills. The rocky surfaces of the hills are adorned with thousands of rock paintings, some of which are estimated to be over 13,000 years old. These paintings depict a wide range of subjects, from scenes of hunting and dancing to intricate patterns and abstract symbols.

The rock art of the Matobo Hills is a testament to the spiritual and cultural significance of this landscape to the San people. These paintings are not only aesthetically remarkable but also serve as a glimpse into the beliefs, rituals, and daily life of these ancient communities.

One of the most famous rock art sites in the Matobo Hills is the Nswatugi Cave, where visitors can view well-preserved paintings that provide a window into the world of the San people. These artworks offer a unique opportunity to connect with the spiritual and cultural heritage of the region.

The Matobo Hills are also associated with the history of the Ndebele people. In the late 19th century, under the leadership of King Mzilikazi and later his son King Lobengula, the Ndebele established their kingdom in the region, making the hills a center of power and authority.

The hills were the site of significant historical events during the colonial period in Zimbabwe. The Battle of the Shangani, a critical conflict during the First Chimurenga (uprising against colonial rule) in 1893, took place in the Matobo Hills. The hills served as a stronghold for the Ndebele resistance against British forces, and the area is dotted with graves and monuments commemorating this pivotal moment in history.

One of the most iconic landmarks in the Matobo Hills is the grave of Cecil John Rhodes, the British colonialist and mining magnate who played a significant role in the colonization of Zimbabwe. His burial site, known as the

"View of the World," is located atop a granite hill and offers breathtaking panoramic views of the surrounding landscape.

The Matobo Hills are not only a treasure trove of history but also a sanctuary for biodiversity. The unique granite formations and the varied vegetation in the area provide habitats for a diverse range of flora and fauna. The hills are home to species like klipspringers, leopards, and rock hyraxes, as well as numerous bird species.

Exploring the Matobo Hills is an adventure that takes visitors on a journey through time, culture, and nature. Whether hiking among the impressive granite outcrops, marveling at ancient rock art, or reflecting on the historical significance of the region, the Matobo Hills offer an experience that is both enlightening and awe-inspiring.

Hwange National Park: Zimbabwe's Wildlife Sanctuary

Hwange National Park, located in the western part of Zimbabwe, is a pristine wilderness that stands as a testament to the country's commitment to wildlife conservation and the preservation of natural heritage. Covering an immense expanse of approximately 14,600 square kilometers (5,600 square miles), Hwange is Zimbabwe's largest national park and one of Africa's premier wildlife sanctuaries.

The park's diverse landscapes encompass everything from vast grasslands to mopane woodlands, teak forests to shallow pans, providing a rich tapestry of habitats that support an astonishing array of wildlife. Hwange National Park has earned its reputation as a haven for some of Africa's most iconic and majestic species.

One of the most remarkable aspects of Hwange is its elephant population. The park is home to one of the largest elephant herds in Africa, with estimates of over 40,000 individuals. These gentle giants roam freely across the park, creating awe-inspiring scenes as they traverse the plains, quench their thirst at waterholes, and strip leaves from acacia trees.

Hwange's elephants are not only a sight to behold but also a symbol of the park's conservation success. The management and protection of these magnificent creatures have been central to Hwange's mission, and the park is renowned for its efforts to mitigate human-elephant conflicts and ensure the coexistence of both species.

The park's impressive diversity extends beyond elephants. Hwange National Park is also home to other members of the "Big Five," including African lions, African leopards, African buffalo, and white rhinoceros. These charismatic animals, along with cheetahs, wild dogs, and various antelope species, create a thriving ecosystem that draws wildlife enthusiasts and photographers from around the world.

One of the defining features of Hwange National Park is its extensive network of waterholes and pans, particularly during the dry season. These water sources are a lifeline for the park's inhabitants, attracting a staggering variety of animals, from predators to prey. The sight of lions, hyenas, and leopards converging on a waterhole in the golden light of dawn or dusk is a captivating spectacle for safari-goers.

Hwange is renowned for its rich birdlife as well, with over 400 bird species recorded within its borders. From majestic raptors like African fish eagles and martial eagles to the vibrant plumage of lilac-breasted rollers and bee-eaters, the park offers a birdwatcher's paradise.

Visitors to Hwange National Park have the opportunity to explore its vast landscapes through guided safaris, game drives, and walking safaris. Experienced guides lead travelers on journeys of discovery, providing insights into the park's ecology, tracking wildlife, and sharing their knowledge of the flora and fauna that make Hwange a unique and special place.

The experience of staying in Hwange is also a memorable one, with a variety of lodges, tented camps, and safari accommodations offering comfort and immersion in the natural surroundings. Many of these lodges are strategically positioned near waterholes, providing guests with a front-row seat to the wildlife spectacle that unfolds each day.

Hwange National Park is not only a sanctuary for wildlife but also a testament to Zimbabwe's commitment to conservation and sustainable tourism. The park is managed by the Zimbabwe Parks and Wildlife Management Authority, which plays a critical role in safeguarding its natural heritage.

Conservation challenges, including poaching and habitat loss, persist in the region, but Hwange's dedicated rangers and conservationists work tirelessly to protect the park's inhabitants and habitats. The park also benefits from international support and cooperation, reflecting the global importance of preserving Africa's natural treasures.

In conclusion, Hwange National Park is a living testament to the splendor and diversity of Africa's wildlife. Its vast landscapes, thriving ecosystems, and charismatic species make it a destination of choice for wildlife enthusiasts and conservationists. Hwange's enduring legacy as a wildlife sanctuary reflects the harmony between humans and nature and serves as an inspiration for the conservation efforts that will ensure its beauty and biodiversity endure for generations to come.

Great Zimbabwe National Monument: UNESCO World Heritage

Great Zimbabwe National Monument, situated in the southeastern part of Zimbabwe, is a place of profound historical and archaeological significance. This UNESCO World Heritage Site, often referred to simply as "Great Zimbabwe," stands as a testament to the architectural and engineering prowess of ancient African civilizations and serves as a symbol of national pride and identity.

The name "Great Zimbabwe" is derived from the Shona words "dzimba dza mabwe," which can be translated to mean "houses of stone" or "stone buildings." These stone structures, built without the use of mortar, are a defining feature of the monument and are a source of fascination for visitors and scholars alike.

The history of Great Zimbabwe dates back to around the 11th century when the construction of the monument is believed to have begun. It reached its zenith between the 13th and 15th centuries during the height of the Shona civilization. Great Zimbabwe served as the capital of a powerful kingdom and was a hub of trade, culture, and political authority in the region.

One of the most iconic features of Great Zimbabwe is the Great Enclosure, a massive stone-walled structure that served various functions, including potentially being a royal residence or a symbolic center of power. The Great Enclosure is adorned with a striking conical tower, often referred to as the "Tower of Great Zimbabwe," which has become an emblematic representation of the monument.

Great Zimbabwe's stone structures are a testament to the advanced architectural and engineering skills of its builders. The precision with which the stones were cut and stacked without the use of mortar is a marvel that continues to puzzle experts. The granite blocks, some weighing several tons, were meticulously shaped and fitted together with astonishing accuracy.

The monument also features an extensive system of dry-stone walls, passageways, and terraces that are indicative of complex urban planning and engineering. The walls serve various purposes, from delineating different areas within the site to providing defensive structures. The craftsmanship exhibited in these walls is a testament to the sophistication of the society that built them.

Great Zimbabwe's historical significance extends beyond its impressive architecture. It was a thriving center of trade, connecting the inland regions of southern Africa with the coastal trade routes of the Indian Ocean. Archaeological evidence, including artifacts such as pottery, glass beads, and gold objects, attests to the exchange of goods and ideas that took place here.

The gold trade, in particular, played a pivotal role in the wealth and influence of Great Zimbabwe. The kingdom's control over gold resources in the region contributed to its prosperity and made it a key player in regional trade networks.

The decline of Great Zimbabwe, which began in the 15th century, is a topic of ongoing debate among historians and archaeologists. Factors such as environmental changes, shifts in trade routes, and political upheaval have all been proposed as potential causes. The exact circumstances that led to the abandonment of Great Zimbabwe and the dispersal of its population remain subjects of research and exploration.

Great Zimbabwe National Monument was declared a UNESCO World Heritage Site in 1986 in recognition of its cultural and historical significance. The site's inclusion on the World Heritage List underscores its importance as a place of global importance that merits protection and preservation for future generations.

Today, Great Zimbabwe stands as a source of national pride for Zimbabweans and a symbol of the country's rich heritage. It is also a destination for travelers and scholars who come to marvel at its remarkable stone structures, explore its archaeological mysteries, and gain insights into the complex history of southern Africa.

In conclusion, Great Zimbabwe National Monument is a treasure trove of history, culture, and architectural achievement. Its stone structures, built by an ancient civilization, continue to captivate and inspire awe. As a UNESCO World Heritage Site, it represents not only Zimbabwe's heritage but also the shared heritage of humanity, reminding us of the enduring legacy of Africa's great civilizations and the importance of preserving our collective past.

Harare: From Salisbury to Modern Capital

Harare, the vibrant capital city of Zimbabwe, is a place of historical significance, cultural diversity, and evolving urban landscapes. Its journey from a colonial outpost known as Salisbury to a modern and cosmopolitan capital reflects the complex history and resilience of the nation.

The story of Harare's transformation begins with the colonial era. In the late 19th century, British settlers established a presence in the region that would become Zimbabwe. In 1890, the city was founded as Salisbury, named after the British Prime Minister, Lord Salisbury. Under British colonial rule, the city served as the administrative and political center of Southern Rhodesia.

Salisbury's early years were marked by rapid growth and development, driven by the discovery of gold and the influx of European settlers. The city's layout and architecture reflected the colonial influence, with wide boulevards, government buildings, and elegant homes.

However, this period of growth and prosperity was accompanied by racial segregation and the disenfranchisement of the indigenous population. The policies of apartheid and racial discrimination that prevailed in Salisbury, as in the rest of Southern Rhodesia, were a source of deep-seated tensions and injustices.

In the midst of these challenges, the struggle for independence began to gain momentum. The city became a focal point for political activism and resistance against colonial rule. The University of Rhodesia (now the University of Zimbabwe) became a hotbed of anti-colonial activism and played a pivotal role in shaping the country's future.

The transformation of Salisbury into Harare was emblematic of the broader transformation taking place in the country. On April 18, 1982, following Zimbabwe's independence in 1980, the city was officially renamed Harare. The name "Harare" is derived from the Shona chieftain Neharawa, whose village was located near the present-day city.

Independence marked a turning point in the city's history. Harare became not only the political capital but also the economic, cultural, and social heart of the newly formed nation. It embraced a vision of inclusivity, multiculturalism, and reconciliation, seeking to bridge the divides of the past.

The city's skyline began to change as modern buildings and infrastructure projects emerged. Harare's streets, once segregated, became symbols of unity as people from diverse backgrounds and ethnicities came together to build a new Zimbabwe.

Harare's cultural diversity is reflected in its neighborhoods, each with its unique character and communities. Suburbs like Avondale, Borrowdale, and Highlands offer a mix of residential, commercial, and cultural experiences. The Avenues, known for their tree-lined streets, host a range of medical facilities and services. The city's green spaces, such as Harare Gardens and the National Botanic Gardens, provide places of relaxation and recreation for residents and visitors. The Kopje, a prominent granite hill in the city center, offers panoramic views of Harare and a glimpse into the city's geological history.

Harare's vibrant arts and cultural scene have earned it a reputation as a hub for creativity and expression. The National Gallery of Zimbabwe showcases the work of local and international artists, while theaters like Theatre in the Park and Reps Theatre offer a platform for performing arts.

Education plays a vital role in the city's life, with a range of schools, colleges, and universities offering diverse educational opportunities. The University of Zimbabwe, founded during the colonial era, remains a center of excellence in higher education.

Harare's economy is diverse and dynamic, with sectors ranging from finance and commerce to agriculture and manufacturing. The city's central business district is a bustling hub of activity, housing financial institutions, government offices, and commercial enterprises.

While Harare has faced its share of challenges, including economic fluctuations and political developments, it continues to evolve and adapt. Its people, known for their resilience and creativity, play a central role in shaping its future.

Harare is a city that reflects the tapestry of Zimbabwe's history, from its colonial past to its post-independence journey towards a more inclusive and prosperous future. As the capital of a nation with a rich cultural heritage and a commitment to progress, Harare remains a place of dynamic change and enduring hope.

Bulawayo: Zimbabwe's Second City

Bulawayo, often referred to as the "City of Kings," holds a distinct and significant place in the tapestry of Zimbabwean history and urban development. As the country's second-largest city, Bulawayo has a rich and complex story that spans centuries, from its precolonial origins to its role as a dynamic and evolving urban center in contemporary Zimbabwe.

The roots of Bulawayo's history reach back to the Ndebele people, led by King Lobengula, who established their capital here in the 19th century. The city's name, "Bulawayo," is derived from the Ndebele words "bulala" and "wayo," which together mean "the place of slaughter." It is a reference to the site where King Lobengula's warriors would conduct the ritual slaying of cattle to honor their ancestors.

The arrival of European settlers in the late 19th century transformed Bulawayo's landscape and set the stage for its growth. Under British colonial rule, the city became a hub of administration, commerce, and industry. Its strategic location as a railway terminus connecting the country's interior with the port of Beira in Mozambique fueled its development.

Bulawayo's early years were characterized by the rapid expansion of its infrastructure and institutions. The city's grid layout, with wide streets and parks, reflected the urban planning ideals of the time. Stately government buildings, churches, and schools emerged, shaping the city's architectural identity.

One of Bulawayo's enduring landmarks is the Bulawayo Railway Station, an architectural gem that stands as a testament to the city's historical significance as a railway hub. Its colonial-era design and grandeur make it an iconic symbol of the city's past.

Bulawayo also played a pivotal role in the development of Zimbabwe's industrial sector. It became home to manufacturing industries, including textiles, food processing, and engineering. These industries contributed to the city's economic vitality and provided employment opportunities for its residents.

Culturally, Bulawayo has been a melting pot of influences. It is often celebrated for its vibrant arts scene, with theaters like the Bulawayo Theatre and Amakhosi Theatre Company serving as venues for the performing arts. The city has produced renowned writers, musicians, and artists who have made significant contributions to Zimbabwean culture.

Bulawayo's diverse neighborhoods offer a glimpse into its multicultural fabric. Suburbs like Hillside, Famona, and North End have distinct characters and demographics. The city's residents, representing a variety of ethnic backgrounds, contribute to its rich cultural mosaic.

The educational landscape of Bulawayo includes a range of schools, colleges, and institutions. Girls' High School and Christian Brothers College are among the city's esteemed educational establishments. The National University of Science and Technology (NUST) is a prominent institution of higher learning located in the city.

The city's green spaces, including Centenary Park and the Bulawayo Golf Club, provide opportunities for relaxation and recreation. The Matobo National Park, a UNESCO World Heritage Site known for its striking rock formations and ancient rock art, is within driving distance from Bulawayo.

In recent years, Bulawayo has faced economic challenges and infrastructural issues, mirroring broader national trends. However, the city's residents have shown resilience and innovation in the face of these challenges, with community initiatives and cultural events continuing to thrive.

Bulawayo remains an integral part of Zimbabwe's urban landscape, with a rich history, cultural vibrancy, and a resilient spirit. As the "City of Kings," it carries forward the legacy of its Ndebele roots while embracing the diversity and dynamism of modern Zimbabwe. Bulawayo's story is one of transformation, adaptation, and the enduring spirit of its people in the face of change.

Gweru: The Heart of the Midlands

Gweru, a city nestled in the heart of Zimbabwe's Midlands Province, exudes a unique charm and character that make it a compelling part of the country's urban landscape. This city, often referred to as "Gweru," is a place where history, industry, and natural beauty converge to create a dynamic and evolving urban center.

The origins of Gweru can be traced back to the 1890s when European settlers, under British colonial rule, established the town as a stop along the railway line connecting the southern city of Bulawayo to the capital, Salisbury (now Harare). The city's strategic location as a railway junction contributed significantly to its growth and development.

Gweru's early years were marked by its role as an essential transportation hub, facilitating the movement of goods and people across the country. The railway station, a central landmark in the city, reflects this history and serves as a reminder of Gweru's significance in Zimbabwe's transportation network.

The city's name, "Gweru," is derived from the Shona word "gweru," which means "small wild cucumber." This indigenous plant, found in the region, is a symbol of the city's natural surroundings and serves as a testament to the local flora.

Gweru is often referred to as the "City of Progress," reflecting its commitment to growth and development. The city's layout features wide streets, tree-lined avenues, and parks that provide a sense of spaciousness and greenery. Its architectural landscape includes a mix of colonial-era buildings and more modern structures, showcasing the city's historical and evolving character.

The Midlands Hotel, a prominent establishment in Gweru, has played a central role in the city's social and cultural life. It is a place where residents and visitors gather for meals, socializing, and events, creating a sense of community and tradition.

Education has been a cornerstone of Gweru's identity, with several educational institutions serving the city and its surrounding areas. Midlands State University (MSU), one of Zimbabwe's leading universities, is located in Gweru and has contributed to the city's reputation as an educational center.

The city's economy has diversified over the years, with sectors such as agriculture, manufacturing, and commerce playing vital roles. Gweru has a strong agricultural presence, with farming activities in the surrounding areas supporting the local economy. The city also hosts industrial facilities and commercial enterprises that contribute to its economic vitality.

Gweru's cultural scene thrives through various initiatives and events, including music festivals, art exhibitions, and theater productions. The city has produced talented artists, musicians, and writers who have contributed to Zimbabwe's cultural heritage.

Natural beauty surrounds Gweru, with nearby attractions such as the Antelope Park, a wildlife conservation and adventure center, providing opportunities for visitors to connect with nature and wildlife. The Gweru River meanders through the city, adding to its scenic charm.

Over the years, Gweru has faced its share of challenges, including economic fluctuations and infrastructure development needs. However, its residents have demonstrated resilience and a commitment to progress, with community initiatives and civic engagement driving positive change.

Gweru's role as a regional center continues to evolve, with ongoing efforts to promote tourism, economic growth, and cultural exchange. As the "Heart of the Midlands," the city embraces its heritage, welcomes diversity, and looks towards a future of continued development and prosperity. Gweru's story is one of growth, adaptability, and the enduring spirit of its people in the heart of Zimbabwe's Midlands Province.

Masvingo: Gateway to Great Zimbabwe

Masvingo, a city steeped in history and culture, serves as the gateway to one of Zimbabwe's most iconic and enigmatic landmarks, Great Zimbabwe. Located in the southeastern part of the country, Masvingo, formerly known as Fort Victoria, is a place where the past and the present coexist in harmony, offering visitors a glimpse into Zimbabwe's rich heritage.

The city's name, "Masvingo," is derived from the Shona word "Masvingo," meaning "fort." This name harks back to the colonial era when the British established Fort Victoria in the late 19th century as a military outpost and administrative center. Over time, the city has evolved, shedding its colonial past while preserving its historical significance.

Masvingo's central location in Zimbabwe's southeastern region positions it as a vital crossroads for travelers heading to Great Zimbabwe National Monument, a UNESCO World Heritage Site located just a few kilometers away. Great Zimbabwe, often referred to as the "Stone City," is a collection of ancient stone structures built by an advanced African civilization between the 11th and 15th centuries. The site has captured the imagination of archaeologists, historians, and tourists for generations.

One of the most remarkable features of Great Zimbabwe is the Great Enclosure, a massive stone-walled structure with a conical tower that stands as a symbol of the monument.

Visitors to Masvingo often begin their journey by exploring the enigmatic ruins of Great Zimbabwe, gaining insights into the architectural and engineering marvels of this ancient civilization. The site also provides a glimpse into the cultural, economic, and social aspects of the society that built it.

Masvingo's connection to Great Zimbabwe extends beyond its role as a starting point for visitors. The city itself boasts historical and cultural attractions. The National Heroes Acre, a monument honoring Zimbabwean heroes, stands as a place of remembrance and reflection. The city's vibrant markets, where artisans and traders showcase their wares, offer a taste of local culture and craftsmanship.

Education plays a significant role in Masvingo, with several schools, colleges, and institutions providing educational opportunities to residents and students from neighboring regions. Masvingo Polytechnic College and Great Zimbabwe University are among the educational institutions contributing to the city's intellectual vibrancy.

The city's natural surroundings, including Lake Mutirikwi (formerly Lake Kyle), provide opportunities for outdoor recreation and leisure. The lake, created by the construction of a dam, offers fishing, boating, and picnicking spots for both residents and tourists.

Masvingo's economy has diversified over the years, with agriculture, tourism, and commerce playing key roles. The city's proximity to Great Zimbabwe makes it an ideal base for visitors exploring the region, contributing to the local tourism industry. Agriculture, including cattle ranching and crop farming, remains an essential part of the local economy.

Culturally, Masvingo is a melting pot of traditions and ethnicities, with people from various backgrounds calling it home. This diversity is celebrated through cultural festivals, music, and dance, which reflect the mosaic of Zimbabwean culture.

Mutare: Zimbabwe's Eastern Gem

Nestled in the lush landscapes of Zimbabwe's eastern highlands lies Mutare, a city known for its natural beauty, rich history, and vibrant culture. Mutare, the capital of Manicaland Province, is often referred to as the "City of Kings" due to its location in a region historically associated with royalty. With its scenic surroundings and diverse heritage, Mutare stands as a true gem in the eastern part of Zimbabwe.

The name "Mutare" has its roots in the Shona language, meaning "a place of metal" or "a place where metals are found." This name is a nod to the city's proximity to the rich mineral deposits that have played a significant role in Zimbabwe's economic history.

One of Mutare's most captivating features is its natural beauty. The city is surrounded by the picturesque Eastern Highlands, a region characterized by rolling hills, lush forests, and pristine rivers. The mountains, including the Bvumba Mountains and Nyanga National Park, offer opportunities for hiking, birdwatching, and outdoor adventure.

The Vumba Botanical Gardens, located in the Bvumba Mountains, provide a stunning showcase of indigenous and exotic plant species. The gardens are a haven for nature enthusiasts and a place of tranquility and reflection.

Mutare's geographical proximity to the Mozambique border has contributed to its role as a regional trade and transportation hub. The Forbes Border Post, connecting

Zimbabwe and Mozambique, facilitates the movement of goods and people between the two countries.

The city's history is intertwined with the broader story of Zimbabwe's struggle for independence. During the liberation war, Mutare served as a base for freedom fighters and played a significant role in the resistance against colonial rule.

Mutare's urban landscape combines elements of history and modernity. The city center features a mix of colonial-era buildings, government offices, and commercial establishments. The Mutare Museum, housed in a historic building, showcases the region's archaeological, ethnographic, and natural history artifacts.

Education is a cornerstone of Mutare's identity, with numerous schools, colleges, and institutions offering educational opportunities. Mutare Teachers College and Africa University, a private institution with a Pan-African focus, contribute to the city's educational vibrancy.

The city's diverse population reflects Zimbabwe's multicultural fabric. People from various ethnic backgrounds call Mutare home, contributing to a rich tapestry of languages, traditions, and cultural celebrations.

The economy of Mutare is driven by a mix of sectors, including agriculture, mining, manufacturing, and trade. Agriculture, including horticulture and forestry, thrives in the fertile soils of the Eastern Highlands. The mining industry, with deposits of minerals such as gold and diamonds, has historical significance and continues to play a vital role in the city's economy.

Mutare's cultural scene is vibrant, with music, dance, and traditional ceremonies reflecting the heritage of its residents. The city's markets, such as Sakubva Market, are lively places where artisans and traders showcase their crafts and products.

Kwekwe: Mining and Industrial Heritage

In the heart of Zimbabwe's Midlands Province lies Kwekwe, a city whose history is intricately linked to the mining and industrial heritage that has defined its identity for over a century. Kwekwe, formerly known as Que Que, has a story that revolves around gold, iron, and the indomitable spirit of its people.

The name "Kwekwe" is believed to be an onomatopoeic representation of the sound that a hammer makes when striking metal, a fitting name for a city with a strong industrial and mining legacy.

Kwekwe's history as a mining town dates back to the late 19th century when gold was discovered in the area. This discovery led to the establishment of the Que Que Gold Mine, which became one of the most significant gold producers in the country during its heyday. Gold mining in Kwekwe attracted prospectors and fortune seekers, shaping the city's early development.

The presence of gold mines in Kwekwe played a crucial role in Zimbabwe's economic development during the colonial era. Gold from Kwekwe and surrounding mines contributed significantly to British colonial revenues. The city's mineral wealth helped fund the construction of infrastructure such as railways and roads.

Kwekwe's mining heritage is still visible today, with remnants of old mines, shafts, and mining equipment serving as historical landmarks. The Roasting Plant Chimney, a towering structure, stands as a testament to the city's mining past. It was once used for roasting gold ore to extract the precious metal.

Ironically, Kwekwe's mining history also had a dark side, as the city was once notorious for its asbestos mining. Asbestos, a mineral with serious health risks, was extensively mined in the region, resulting in health challenges for miners and environmental concerns.

The city's industrial sector, which grew in tandem with mining, includes manufacturing and foundry activities. Kwekwe's industrial base produced a range of products, including machinery, steel, and building materials. The city was known for its foundries and workshops, contributing to the national industrial landscape.

Kwekwe's economic fortunes have fluctuated over the years, mirroring the broader challenges faced by Zimbabwe's economy. The closure of some mines and industrial facilities in the late 20th century had an impact on the city's employment and economic prospects.

Education has always been a priority in Kwekwe, with schools, colleges, and vocational institutions serving the city's residents. The city is home to Kwekwe High School, a well-regarded educational institution.

Culturally, Kwekwe is a diverse city, with people from various backgrounds living and working together. The city's residents celebrate their heritage through music, dance, and cultural festivals that reflect the mosaic of Zimbabwean culture.

Kwekwe's central location in the Midlands Province makes it a strategic transportation and trade hub, connecting the region to other parts of the country. The city's road and rail networks facilitate the movement of goods and people.

While Kwekwe's mining and industrial heritage remain integral to its identity, the city has also diversified its economy in recent years. Agriculture, commerce, and small-scale mining have emerged as additional economic activities.

As Kwekwe continues its journey into the 21st century, it faces the challenges of adapting to changing economic landscapes and environmental considerations. The city's mining and industrial heritage are both a source of pride and a reminder of the need for sustainable development and responsible resource management.

Kariba: The Lake and the Dam

Nestled in the northwestern corner of Zimbabwe lies the town of Kariba, a place intimately connected to one of Africa's most ambitious engineering projects—the Kariba Dam. Kariba, set on the southern shores of Lake Kariba, is a testament to human ingenuity and the transformation of a once-wild river into a vast, man-made lake that has left an indelible mark on Zimbabwe's landscape.

The name "Kariba" is synonymous with the massive reservoir and the town that emerged as a result of its construction. This engineering marvel, often referred to as the Kariba Hydroelectric Scheme, was born out of a collaborative effort between Zimbabwe and its northern neighbor, Zambia. It was designed not only to generate electricity but also to tame the mighty Zambezi River, which had a history of seasonal flooding.

The idea for the Kariba Dam and Lake Kariba began to take shape in the mid-20th century. The ambitious project was undertaken primarily for the generation of hydroelectric power, which would fuel both Zimbabwe's and Zambia's growing industrial and domestic needs. The dam was envisioned as a means to control the Zambezi River's flow, mitigating the destructive floods that had plagued the region.

Construction of the Kariba Dam commenced in the late 1950s, a colossal endeavor that involved the labor of thousands of workers from both Zimbabwe and Zambia. The sheer scale of the project, which included the construction of the dam wall and associated infrastructure, required intricate planning and engineering expertise. The dam wall itself, towering over 420 feet (128 meters) above the riverbed, became a symbol of human achievement.

The completion of the Kariba Dam in 1959 marked a historic moment for both countries. Lake Kariba, with its capacity to hold an immense volume of water, began to form behind the dam wall. The creation of this artificial lake not only tamed the Zambezi River but also led to the displacement of communities and the submergence of land, altering the local geography forever.

Lake Kariba's significance extends beyond its role in electricity generation and flood control. It became a reservoir teeming with diverse aquatic life, and its waters soon became home to numerous fish species, including the iconic tigerfish. The lake also offers recreational opportunities, such as boating, fishing, and wildlife viewing along its shoreline.

The Kariba Hydroelectric Power Station, with its six generating units, produces a substantial portion of Zimbabwe's electricity. The power station's capacity has made it a vital contributor to the country's energy grid, supporting industrial operations and households across Zimbabwe.

The town of Kariba, which emerged as a result of the dam's construction, serves as a hub for tourism and a gateway to Lake Kariba's wonders. Visitors flock to Kariba to explore the lake's pristine waters, islands, and national parks. Matusadona National Park, situated on the lake's shoreline, is renowned for its wildlife, including elephants, lions, and buffalo.

Zimbabwe Today: Challenges and Aspirations

In the present day, Zimbabwe stands at a crossroads, a nation with a complex and storied past, facing a multitude of challenges and harboring aspirations for a brighter future. The trajectory of the country's recent history, marked by periods of hope and adversity, has shaped its current circumstances.

One of the foremost challenges Zimbabwe grapples with is its economic situation. The country has experienced periods of hyperinflation and currency devaluation, leading to economic instability that has deeply affected the lives of its citizens. Efforts to stabilize the economy and restore investor confidence remain ongoing.

Agriculture, once the backbone of Zimbabwe's economy, has faced challenges, including land reform policies that reshaped the distribution of agricultural land. The transition in land ownership has had both intended and unintended consequences on food production and the agricultural sector.

Zimbabwe's political landscape has also been marked by significant developments. The early 21st century witnessed political transitions and shifts in leadership. The country navigated a challenging path towards establishing a more inclusive and democratic political system.

Human rights and governance issues have been central to Zimbabwe's contemporary narrative. Concerns regarding civil liberties, press freedom, and political stability have been points of contention both domestically and internationally.

Despite these challenges, Zimbabwe remains a nation with immense potential. Its natural resources, including minerals, fertile lands, and a diverse range of ecosystems, offer opportunities for economic growth and environmental conservation.

The people of Zimbabwe, known for their resilience and determination, aspire to see their nation prosper and thrive. Investments in education, healthcare, and infrastructure are crucial steps toward achieving these aspirations.

Tourism has emerged as a promising sector, with Zimbabwe's natural wonders, such as Victoria Falls, Hwange National Park, and Matobo Hills, attracting visitors from around the world. The tourism industry contributes to both economic growth and the conservation of the country's rich biodiversity.

Efforts to address social challenges, such as healthcare access and education quality, remain ongoing priorities. Zimbabwe's healthcare system has been tested by various factors, including disease outbreaks and limited resources.

Zimbabweans are known for their vibrant culture, which includes diverse languages, music, dance, and art. Cultural preservation and promotion are integral to the nation's identity.

The international community plays a role in Zimbabwe's journey, providing support for development initiatives, humanitarian efforts, and diplomatic engagement.

Zimbabwe's future is shaped by the collective determination of its people and leaders to address challenges, embrace opportunities, and build a nation that reflects the aspirations of all its citizens. The nation's story continues to be written, with each chapter revealing the resilience and spirit of Zimbabweans as they navigate the complex landscape of the present while holding onto hopes for a brighter tomorrow.

Conclusion

In the pages of this book, we have embarked on a journey through the annals of time, tracing the rich and complex history of Zimbabwe. From its ancient civilizations to its modern-day challenges and aspirations, Zimbabwe's story is one of resilience, diversity, and enduring hope.

We began by delving into the origins of Zimbabwe, exploring the early inhabitants and cultures that thrived in this land. The rise of Great Zimbabwe, an enigmatic stone city that stands as a testament to the engineering prowess of its builders, captured our imaginations. We journeyed through the kingdoms of Mapungubwe and Khami, witnessing the ebb and flow of power and influence in ancient Zimbabwe.

The rise of the Rozvi Empire and the enduring legacies of the Shona and Ndebele peoples further enriched our understanding of Zimbabwe's history. The advent of Arab traders and Swahili influence brought new connections and cultural exchanges to this landlocked nation.

We marveled at the medieval empire of Monomotapa and delved into the architectural mysteries of Great Zimbabwe. Trade routes and Indian Ocean connections expanded our view of Zimbabwe's place in the global network of commerce.

The arrival of European explorers and the clash of cultures with Portuguese colonialists marked a turning point in Zimbabwe's history. The Mutapa Empire's golden age showcased the heights of indigenous African governance and prosperity.

The impact of the transatlantic slave trade left indelible scars on Zimbabwe's history, as did the era of colonial rule and the complex land question that continues to shape the nation's landscape.

The struggles for independence, known as the Chimurenga Wars, were a testament to the unyielding spirit of Zimbabweans who fought for self-determination and freedom. The birth of modern Zimbabwe under the leadership of Robert Mugabe marked a new chapter in the nation's history.

We explored the legacy of liberation movements and the ongoing challenges and aspirations that define Zimbabwe today. The nation's wildlife and conservation efforts, as well as its savory cuisine, offer glimpses into its natural beauty and cultural richness.

We marveled at the grand spectacle of Victoria Falls, the ancient rock art and history of Matobo Hills, and the wildlife sanctuary of Hwange National Park. The Great Zimbabwe National Monument, a UNESCO World Heritage Site, stands as a testament to the enduring legacy of this nation's past.

We ventured into the modern capitals of Harare and Bulawayo, explored the heart of the Midlands in Gweru, and discovered the gateway to Great Zimbabwe in Masvingo. Mutare, in the eastern highlands, offered us a glimpse into the city's mining and industrial heritage, while Kwekwe showcased the history of mining and industry.

Kariba, with its lake and dam, exemplified human engineering and the transformation of landscapes. Finally, we reflected on Zimbabwe today, with its challenges and aspirations, and the resilience of its people in the face of adversity.

As we conclude this journey through the history of Zimbabwe, we are reminded that this nation's story is still being written. Zimbabweans, with their rich cultural heritage, boundless determination, and enduring hope, continue to shape their destiny. The challenges of the past and present are met with a spirit of unity and a vision of a brighter future.

Zimbabwe's history is a tapestry of triumphs and tribulations, of civilizations risen and empires fallen. It is a testament to the indomitable human spirit, the power of culture, and the pursuit of progress.

Thank you for taking the time to read this book on the history of Zimbabwe. We hope that you found it informative, engaging, and enriching. Your interest in exploring the rich tapestry of Zimbabwe's past is greatly appreciated.

If you enjoyed this book and found it valuable, we kindly request that you consider leaving a positive review. Your feedback is invaluable and helps others discover and appreciate the content.

Your review can be a testament to the effort and dedication that went into creating this book. It also serves as encouragement to continue producing high-quality, informative content for readers like you.

Once again, thank you for your time and interest. Your support is greatly appreciated, and we look forward to hearing your thoughts in the form of a positive review.

Made in United States
Troutdale, OR
08/14/2024

22006484R00056